Go to an Art Gallery or Museum
Un-contacted Tribes
Hangman
Water Gel Beads
Balloons
Computer Games
Monster
Headgear
Quiz
Starting calls in unusual ways
Bedtime stories
Nothing between the ears
Old friends
Hide and seek with toys
Interview a relative
Once Upon a Time
Special Occasions
List of things to do for your next visit
Involving other people
Visit the Zoo
Simon Says
Colouring, scrap and sticker books
Sing a song or a nursery rhyme
Come closer raspberries
The Easter Bunny
Giant Gummy Bear
Photos, video and old scrapbooks
Rhyme Time
The On / Off Switch
My Word
Telling stories about your time together
Treasure Hunt
Two way Jenga
Cups and coin trick
Watching a Show Together
Magic Trees

Dedication

To my children. Distance separates us, but my heart is always with you.

2nd Edition

This is the second edition of a book I first published in 2017. Since then, my children have gotten older and technology has changed faster than ever.

Technological changes are covered in this 2nd Edition, and activities from the first edition are complimented with new ideas and suggestions gathered over the past few years. I hope you enjoy it, and find it useful for making meaningful contact with your loved ones.

:)

Ted

Introduction

Before we get stuck in, let's just pause for a moment and think about the word 'contact'. After all, it is the one word which this book is all about but where it's meaning is often confused or overlooked. In the case of separated parents and grandparents it has come to be associated with legal jargon about access, time constraints and rights. But a child doesn't understand the time they spend with their parents in this way and nor should we.

The word 'contact' in it's truest sense, is the moment of excitement and surprise when you find someone when playing hide and seek. It's the tension and laughter when someone moves playing musical statues. It is the moment you turn up on the doorstep to pick the kids up, dressed as a medieval knight. It is the moments that you and they will always remember.

And it doesn't have to be physical. Contact also happens when somebody reaches out to you with carefully chosen words and pictures in a letter or an email. It happens when telling a funny story on the telephone, and it happens more and more frequently in our electronically connected world by video calling.

I'm sure we can all think of a parent or two who doesn't seem to have good contact with their kids even though they live under the same roof. That should come as no surprise. Good contact after all, is not about how much time you spend together but what you do with it. As a distance parent or grandparent, remember that contact with your children is not just about turning up on a call, it's about the fun of getting involved in activities that can make those special moments happen. And that is where I hope this book will help.

However you use it, and whatever you get up to, have fun and enjoy making memories with your little people!

How to Use This Book

The Distance Contact Bible has been written in short bite-size sections so you can quickly and easily browse for something to do in as little as 5 minutes before a Skype session. Everything you will need to complete an activity is included in the Resources section at the bottom of each page, along with 'Difficulty level' and 'Preparation time' required.

The General Advice section contains all the information you will need to get started. It is recommended that you take time to read through this section first, especially if you are new to video calling.

A Final Word

I once heard someone say, 'If life serves you lemons, make lemonade.' Being served Distance Contact can feel like being served lemons, but over the past 8 years, I have made lemonade, and so can you.

With a little patience and persistence, good relationships can be made, maintained and even improved, despite the miles that come between us. By following this guide book and getting involved in the activities contained within, you'll be on the way to making lemonade in no time.

This is the second edition of the Distance Contact Bible and the update comes at a time when many of us need the help and advice contained within it, more than ever If you have any general feedback, or would like to share activities and success stories please email tedrosetwice@gmail.com - I would love to hear from you!

Section 1

General Advice

Equipment, timing and regularity, and more…

Skype, Google Hangouts, Facetime, Whats App, Snapchat, Messenger, Zoom etc.

Since the first edition of this book, What's App, Snapchat, Messenger and Zoom have emerged alongside the established players such as Skype for video calling. Google Hangouts has been joined by Google Duo which has some pretty impressive features, especially for chatting with kids, and Facetime alongside Messages offers some very cool ways of communicating between Apple devices.

What's app, Facebook Messenger and FaceTime have become the go-to's for video calling on mobile devices, and Zoom has taken over the business end of video calling.

AR (augmented reality) features have evolved too, such that Snapchat, Messenger, FaceTime and Google Duo now come with some really fun features that allow you to do all sorts of crazy things to your face which the kids will enjoy (my daughter absolutely loves it when I wear the Octopus face using Facetime)

What's App is my go-to for calling with my son, and occasionally we use Snapchat now that he's old enough to have his own phone. The app you end up using will likely be the one that is most convenient for you both, and depend on the devices being used.

Time of Day for Video Calls

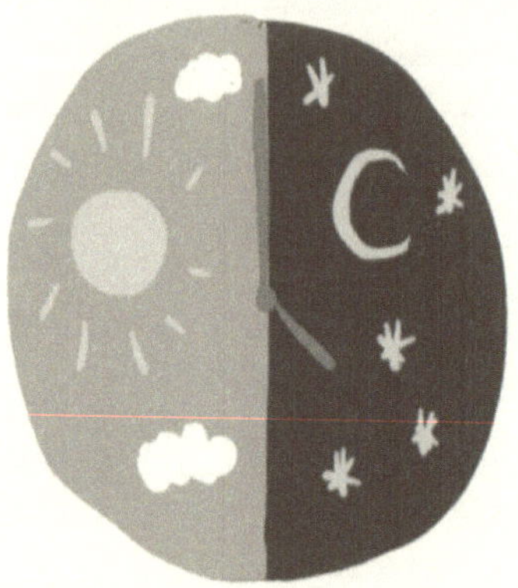

When to video call is going to depend on a few different factors, like your schedule and theirs. If you are at home for most of the week and they are not yet at school, you have lots of flexibility to find a time that works best for you and your children. If you don't have that luxury, you are probably going to be restricted to morning and evening.

If you live in the same time zone that shouldn't be too much of a problem. Similarly, if you live on the opposite side of the world, things should work out reasonably well, as their morning will be your evening and vice-versa. The problems may start to occur when you are around 3-6 hours ahead or behind because this will mean that you either have to get up early in the morning or stay up late at night if you want to video-call on weekdays (assuming you are both at work and school). Weekends shouldn't be a problem of course, so it may be that you end up doing a short video or phone call or two in the week, and then a longer one at the weekend.

Being restricted to morning and evening is no bad thing, but do bear in mind that they will be very different types of video-calls. Morning for them will be boisterous and it's a good time to get involved in most of the activities contained in this book. By evening, they may be getting tired and irritable, so even though you might still be able to have some fun, it may be best to focus on questions about their day or bed-time stories.

Everybody is different however, so try different things until you find a format that works for everyone. Once you have found your magic formula, stick to it. Predictability and routine is important for kids and adults so groove it until everyone knows where they stand, and video-calling becomes a habit that you and your kids continue to enjoy into the future.

Regularity of Video Calls

One of the most important things to get right from the start is how often you intend to call. This will vary depending on your circumstances. Once every month or two might work quite well for non-custodial grandparents, but for a long distance parent, at least once a week would likely be more appropriate. Proof of the importance of regular calls is contained in this personal anecdote - having not had physical contact with my young children for close to 2 years, there were question marks over how our first meeting would go. Everybody was nervous, and nobody quite knew what to expect. In the end, our transition from digital contact to the real life was pretty seamless, which surprised everyone except my new partner, who said, 'You know why it was so easy for you and the kids don't you? Because you maintained such good, regular contact.'

And she was right! Grooving regular calls is good for everybody concerned - parents and grandparents know where they stand and what is expected of them and kids benefit from the certainty of knowing that they will see you regularly.

Whatever you decide, whether it's one to three times a week for long-distance parents or once every month or so for grandparents, keep at it if you want to maintain a good relationship with your kids from afar.

Length of Video Calls

The length of a call will depend on a number of factors, such as age of the children, their schedule and yours and how energetic you're all feeling. My best advice here is to fix regular times during the week but to be as flexible as possible - read the signs and make it longer if it's going well and shorter if anybody is tired or irritable. Generally, I try to keep calls at least 5 to 10 minutes in length, and that would be an appropriate amount of time for babies and toddlers who have much shorter attention spans. My average over two calls per week would be around 30 minutes to 1 hour each call. Occasionally a call might go on for two hours or more, but those are exceptions to the rule and usually involve lots of downtime where one or other of us is doing something like drawing or colouring pictures. If you aren't a Long Distance Parent or if you do video-calls more or less frequently you might want to play with those numbers a bit until you find something that works best for you and your children.

The reason why I find that 30 minutes to 1 hour works well for us is because over that length of time, we are most probably going to have good 'contact' with each other at some point. The problem is that it's hard to predict when that point will be - sometimes things start slowly with both sides possibly a bit distracted and disengaged, but then, 5 minutes into the session, something happens, contact is made and it's all go… Conversely, some sessions have started with a hiss and a roar, and then fizzled out.

So use your own judgement, play it by ear a bit, and remember that the aim of the game is to have fun and make real 'contact' regardless of whether it takes 5 minutes or 2 hours.

Devices for Video Calls

Almost any device that is connected to the internet can be used for video calling these days, so which you use depends on where you are and how you connect.

At home, a laptop or desktop computer is good for features, functionality and screen size. On the move, tablets and cellphones offer greater convenience and flexibility.

When deciding which to use, you might also consider that some features will not work (or are very tricky to set up with variable results) on a mobile device - 'video call recording' and 'share screen' being two very useful examples. Features like this are fantastic at home, but not really necessary if you are considering a video-call bicycle ride via a mobile data connection.

Sometimes you may want to use a tablet and desktop together. I do this by drawing something using my electronic pen (stylus) and tablet whilst making the actual video call from my desktop computer. I then either hold my tablet up for them to see or print my Artwork and send it to them in the post.

On the kids side, access to a tablet or iPad means that they can give you a tour of the most recent den they have made, or perhaps show you something they found in the garden, whilst a laptop or desktop machine is easier to tilt and usually has a lot more screen space for a whole range of activities at the kitchen or lounge table.

Note: If you are on a desktop / laptop and they are on a mobile device, you can still share your desktop screen with them, but they will not be able to share their screen with you.

Tips: If your kids don't have access to a tablet and they are old enough, why not make a present of one? Basic Android devices are very cheap these days and available from most online retailers.

Screen Sharing

Screen sharing allows you to share your entire computer screen or a single window with the person you are calling. Since the first edition of this book, technology has changed fast and it is now possible to share your screen from virtually any device.

It is a great feature when video calling kids and as you progress through this book, you will find all sorts of cool activities that involve screen sharing like globetrotting with Google Maps, showing photos and video or reading an eBook together. I play Hangman regularly with my kids which they love, but the possibilities are endless so learn how to do it on your device and get stuck in!

Tips: Screen sharing is possible with most applications, but some are easier to get going than others, with Skype being the easiest.

Resources: Screen sharing software such as Skype and your device

Screenshots

A screenshot captures your computer/tablet screen as you are looking at it just as if you had taken a photo.

If you don't know how to do it, then now is the perfect time to start. It's very easy and a great way of preserving video-call memories. You'll also end up with lots of cool pictures to print out next time you send a parcel in the post!

On a Mac computer there are a couple of keyboard shortcuts you can use depending on how much of the screen you want to take a picture of, but the bog-standard 'take a picture of the whole screen' shortcut is 'Command, Shift, 3'. On an iPad, holding down the power button and the home button saves a screenshot to your photo gallery and on a Windows computer it's 'Alt' (or 'Windows Key') and 'Print Screen'.

Tips: I import screenshots into my drawing application and then use my stylus to draw things like moustaches and hats on my kids, which always ends in fit's of giggles… If you want to have a go at this before showing them your Artwork try saying, 'Now, nobody laugh when I show you this, OK?! You're not going to laugh now are you?' - this builds the suspense and makes them laugh even harder when you eventually show them what you have done!

Resources: The screen shot feature is available on most computers and mobile devices.

Recording Video Calls

Recording video-calls is easy to do and with a one hour session weighing in at around 200Mb (depending on your settings), it's not going to break the bank to store them on a hard drive for you and your kids to enjoy watching again in the
future.

Once you've installed the software, you can set it up to automatically record calls to a folder of your choosing so you'll never have to think about it again - brilliant! Full instructions on how to do this will come with your software's documentation.

Tips: Sometimes it's quite nice to send a freeze-frame of your session to the kids by email or printed out in the post. They'll enjoy being reminded of a funny moment or of something you've done together.

Resources: Ecamm's 'Call recorder' is commonly regarded as the best tool for Skype and I can certainly vouch for it, but there are alternatives, with some of them available for free if you are on a Windows computer.

Props

A box of props is always handy for video-calls. My box contains story books, stuffed toys, guns, balloons, jenga blocks, toy cars, a pirates eyepatch, face-paint and plenty more besides… Some items may become favourites and get used more than others (guns and soft toys for my kids) whilst others gather dust. Whatever your kids preferences, keep your props box evolving, and when it comes to parcel time why not raid the props box and send them one or two items to remind them of the fun you have had together?!

Phone calls, parcels and postcards

Variety is the spice of life, so why not supplement your video-calling schedule with a few old fashioned phone calls here and there! There are lots of free or cheap calling options these days so international phone calls no longer break the bank. Just don't expect too much, or too long on the phone and you'll find that it makes a good addition to your communication toolset.

Other forms of communication like letters, parcels and postcards offer yet more invaluable ways of overcoming the distance barrier and give your children something personal that they can touch and feel.

Tips: Make phone calls fun by pretending you've called the wrong number and that you want to order a Chinese takeaway, or that your the station master from Harry Potter's platform 9 and 3/4 wondering why they're not there ready to board the train?!

Messaging

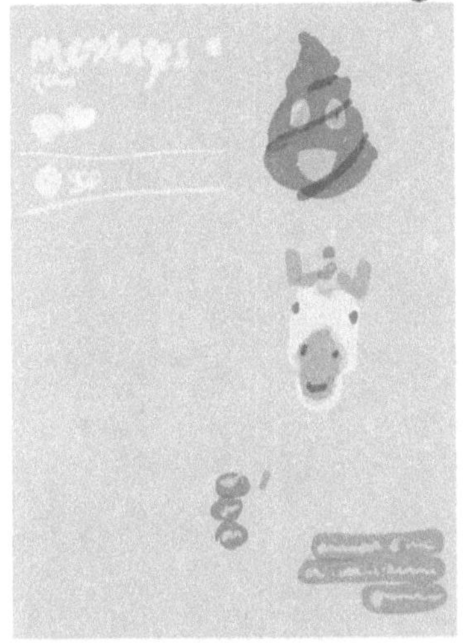

Messaging started out a long time ago with SMS texts on cell phones, but with the advent of apps like Whatsapp, Apple Messages, Messenger and Snapchat, it has evolved into a multi-featured way of making short-form contact in lots of fun ways.

If your little people are old enough to have their own devices and you have the same Apps loaded, you're good to go. If not, you may need an adult on the other side to deliver messages sent to their devices.

With Apps like those mentioned above you can record voice or video greetings, send pictures and photographs, emojis and even try some of the fun new AR (Augmented Reality) features by turning yourself into a talking octopus or an alien!

I use WhatsApp and Snapchat with my son, and Apple Messages with my daughter. Apple messages is probably the most fun, but Snapchat is packed with lots of fun features too.

Augmented Reality

Augmented reality is something that still sounds a bit technical to the older generation, but its actually quite simple and definitely worth knowing about for video calls with kids, which is why I've included it in this 2nd edition.

Most people will be familiar with the idea of a 'selfie' where someone looks like they have added computer generated bunny ears and whiskers to their face? And some of you may have played Pokemon Go or seen Achitectural drawings where an imaginary building is set in an existing landscape? Well, that's AR… What does this mean for you and your video calls? It means you can have fun playing with the AR 'lenses', effects and filters available on apps such as Snapchat, Facebook Messenger and Google Duo, or the really cool Animoji/Memoji features and effects on Apple FaceTime. The lenses and memoji's adjust and move with your face, so if you wink, the Memoji winks, if you're wearing a moustache lens and you move your face, the moustache moves too! My daughter loves me turning up for a call with the Octopus face, which she thinks is very cute (and there was me thinking I was cute without the Octopus face… :)

Resources: A device that can use the AR effects available via apps like

Snapchat, Facebook Messenger, Google Duo and Apple FaceTime.

Preparation Time: Less than 5 minutes

Difficulty level: Easy

School and Homework

Getting into detail about what's happening at school can be difficult with kids, so establishing links directly with teachers or asking your child's main care giver to forward news from school is invaluable for keeping track of your child's educational development.

Armed with this knowledge you can then go on to tailor some of your video-call sessions to help out with maths, reading or whatever other area they need support in. If you are able to get copies of their exercise books, collaborating with them will be easy using the 'screen sharing' feature of your software - just open the document, share your screen and work on the exercises together.

Resources: A desktop computer for screen sharing. A pressure sensitive tablet and stylus will be useful for showing them how to handwrite maths problems or words on screen - it is possible to use a mouse or mousepad to handwrite in a drawing application but it is quite a lot more difficult. If you do not have a drawing application loaded on your machine, www.sketch.io provides a good free browser based alternative.

Babies and toddlers

A baby's attention span is very short, and their understanding of the world is limited, so hoping that you can make a video-call and get involved in all the activities contained within this book is going to end in disengagement and disappointment on both sides. Remember that distance contact with kids at this age is more about reassuring them that you still exist than anything else - it's about the sound of your voice and your face on the screen in front of them. So, try to focus on the stuff that grabs their attention for a moment or two at a time - like pulling a funny face or blowing a raspberry into the microphone… If it works and you're rewarded with a smile, do it again! It's as easy as that.

Bedtime stories are perhaps the exception to this rule - kids take great comfort from the sound of a parent reading as they fall asleep, so if you are able to read to them at bedtime, all the better. If timing is a problem, how about recording some short videos of you reading stories and uploading them to Youtube (you might want to make sure they are 'Unlisted' unless you want the rest of the world to see them!) or send them a USB drive in the post?

As babies develop into toddlers, so does their attention span and you can start to integrate some of the simple activities from the list below for your video-calls, working the occasional activity from the main part of the book in as you go.

Activities for small children / toddlers:

- Hold soft toys or puppets up to the camera. Give them a voice and maybe make up a story for them.
- Do the 'Starting calls in unusual ways' activity.
- Ask an adult to give your child some paper and colouring pens for them to draw a picture while you watch.
- Do the 'Come closer raspberries' activity.
- Play 'Peekaboo' by hiding your face to the left and right of the screen, and then suddenly appearing from another direction (maybe even try from the bottom, or top of the screen!)
- Do the 'Sing a song or nursery rhyme' activity.
- Do the 'Google Hangouts' activity.
- As them to point to different parts of their bodies, like their eyes and nose. Point to yours if they are struggling.
- Use the 'screen sharing' feature to show family photos and video.
- Do the 'On/Off Switch' activity.
- Ask them (or ask an adult for help) to show you their favourite toy. Ask them questions about the toy and make your own comments about it too.
- Do the 'Involving other people' activity.
- Do the 'Squeaky voice / Darth Vader voice' activity.
- Put some music on and dance together!
- Do the 'Dead or Asleep?' activity.

- Do the 'Shoot-outs' activity.
- Read short stories, showing them the pictures as you go.
- Ask them what a donkey or a horse and other animals sounds like. Help them out if they get stuck!
- Do the 'Headgear' activity.
- Ask them to show you what they can make with Jenga, Lego or other building blocks.
- Do the 'Strange noises' activity.
- If they are old enough, hold up letters of the alphabet and ask them to tell you what they are. Help out and be patient if they are interested but struggling. Make basic words like Dad and Mum as they get older and improve.
- Use 'share screen' to watch a children's TV show together.
- Do the 'Balloons' activity.
- On birthdays or special occasions, do the 'Special Occasions' activity.

Older Kids and Teenagers

The scope of this book's advice and activities is focussed mainly on pre-teen kids. Older children and teenagers will no doubt be interested in some of the activities contained within this book, but their own personal interests and preferences will start to have a much greater influence on how you spend your time together online as they get older. Being mindful of these changes and adapting to them will become more important as time goes on.

Activities as such may become less frequent, or more focussed depending on their preferences - a friend of mine finds online chess to be a great way of interacting with his son, enabling time for casual conversation as they play, whilst one mother I very much admire finds pitching in with school projects and trips to the virtual shopping mall works wonders with her daughter.

However the relationship with your child changes as they evolve into young adults, try to stay one step ahead of the game by taking the time to read and understand what to expect and how to interact constructively with teenagers. Collaborating with them online in the development of their identity as young adults will help build solid foundations for a lifelong relationship based upon love and mutual respect.

Fun Endings

Finishing video-calls can sometimes be the most fun part!

My daughter is a bright button and has worked out how to call me using her mum's computer. When I hung up the other day, I had a feeling she would call me back… Sure enough, within 5 seconds she was calling and we were off again… Then, (and this is the fun part) I say, "OK, Bye, I love you!" and then end the call really quickly knowing full well that she won't be able to resist calling back again! This time when I answer, I move out of range of the camera and wait for the 'Dad? Daddy?! Dad, where are you?!" … And then I move my head into the shot sideways and slowly from the left, which she thinks is hilarious… and we're off again!

Tips: When you answer the call for the 8th time, try freezing, or swapping places with a different person, or a cuddly toy… The possibilities are endless!

If your child hasn't worked out how to call you yet, perhaps try getting them

familiar with the interface by asking them to call you. If this turns out to be too tricky, you could try flipping it around and calling them back multiple times,
even though this option might not be as much fun and could annoy the adults in the house!

When it's not working

For whatever reason, sometimes video-calls just doesn't work the way you hope they will. Maybe things have been a bit stressful in the house on their side or maybe you're tired after a long day. Whatever the reason, accept that there's not a great deal you can do about it. It's still important that you show your faces and have some kind of contact, but probably best to keep it short - there is no point in stringing things out if it's hard work, as that's serving nobody. Use your judgement, read the signals and call it quit's when the opportunity arises…. And look forward to next time!

Section 3

Indoor calling

Most of your video-calls will take place indoors, so in this section we'll look at all the different ways you can make calling fun and interesting for them and you.

Around the World

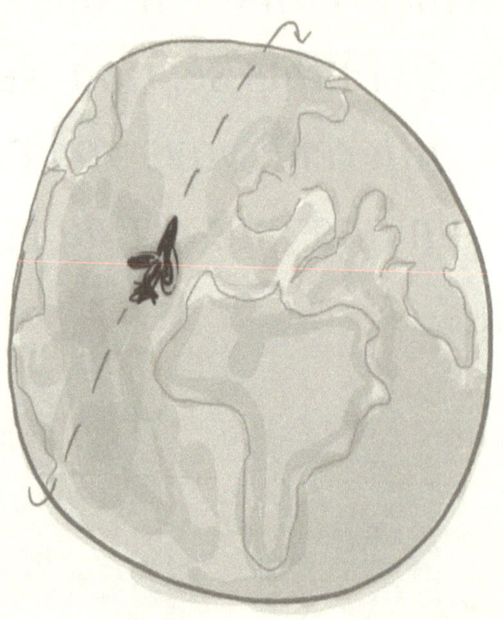

We stumbled upon this activity purely by chance and it works brilliantly well, so well in fact that the day after we tried it for the first time, my son asked excitedly on the telephone if we could do it again next time!
So, what better way to start our activities than with Around the World?
For 'Around the World' you will need a desktop or laptop computer with an App that has screen-sharing functionality, like Skype. Cellphones and tablets will work on their side, but they might not be able to see very well on small screens.

Start the call and 'Share Screen' from the menu. You'll be given the option to share your entire screen or just a window. Select an open internet browser window such as Safari or Chrome to begin sharing. Now, go to your browser and start sharing a map of the world. If you are not sure how to do this, google 'Africa' and select 'Maps' from the options just above the first search result. You are now sharing a map of the world with your kids and can begin your journey together.

Tips:

- Zoom in and out.

- Go to the bottom left of the screen and choose 'Earth' view for satellite imagery.

- Zoom in as far as possible to find their house and show them where you live!

- Enter Google Street view by dragging the little orange man to the street you want to show.

- Ask the kids where they would like to go next and explore the country and it's inhabitants by opening another internet browser tab for them to see.

Around the World is an educational activity that you can return to time and time again. The possibilities are endless, so use your imagination and see where in the world it takes you all!

Resources: A desktop/laptop computer and an App with screen-sharing functionality such as Skype.

Preparation Time: Less than 5 minutes if you are tech-savvy. Add 15 minutes if not.

Difficulty level: Easy

Who am I?

A classic old game that works really well when video-calling. Start by asking your child to think of an animal (but it could be anything, like a fruit or vegetable) but not to tell you what it is. You think of something as well, but don't tell them either. Then ask them to try and guess what type of animal you are by asking a question (for example, 'Do you have a long neck?'). They are only allowed to ask one question and you must either answer Yes, or No. If they get a Yes, they get to ask another question, if they answer No, then you get to ask them a question until you get a No answer. The game ends when somebody guesses who you are!

Tips: This game might be beyond some younger children but give it a go - it's great fun if you can get it going.

Resources: Imagination and your normal video-calling set-up!

Preparation Time: Less than 5 minutes.

Difficulty level: Easy for you to set up. Challenging for them!

Paper bag

This is the kind of activity that your grandmother's grandmother probably did with her kids… All that is required is a paper bag and you're away.

The idea is to come up with as many possible uses for the bag as you can. You might start by drawing a face on it and then blowing it up, or make a hat for a toy bear (or for yourself if it's big enough).

How many ideas can you come up with? How about aiming for 10!

Tips: If you don't have a paper bag handy, try improvising by using sticky tape to make sheets of paper into a bag.

Resources: A paper bag or two on your side and theirs if possible.

Preparation Time: Less than 5 minutes. Add more time if you don't have a paper bag to hand.

Difficulty level: Easy for you to set up. Challenging for them!

Mongolian Throat Singer

Don't ask me how we found Mongolian Throat Singers, we just did!

For this activity, all you need do is google 'Mongolian Throat Singer' and choose one of the videos on YouTube (I like the one with the guy dressed in the ornate green jacket best).

If you are on a desktop machine, why not share your screen, so that the kids can see this unusual cultural delight for themselves?

Why not try stopping the music and doing your own version of the song? It's bound to end up in fit's of giggles!

Tips: Don't stop in Mongolia! Why not search for steel drummers in the Caribean , Digeridoo players in Australia or the pan pipers in South America?

Resources: A desktop computer (if you would like to share your screen)

Preparation Time: Less than 5 minutes if you already know how to 'share screen'

Difficulty level: Easy

The Memory Game

This is an old game that my mum used to play with us when we were children and it works as well for video calls as it did for us in the pre-internet era!

First of all you'll need to collect around 8-10 smallish items from around the house and arrange them on a tray or the table in front of you. Then adjust your webcam so that your children can see the items. Ask them to have a good look and try to remember what they can see on the tray. Now ask them to close their eyes (or turn your webcam off), and whilst they've got their eyes closed take one item from the tray. When they open their eyes again, they have to try and tell you which item has gone! The game carries on until there are no items left on the tray.

Tips: If your kids are struggling with 10 items try reducing the amount of items on your tray to start with until they start getting the hang of the game and developing their memory skills.

Resources: A tray (if you don't have one, a clear space on the table will work as long as you are able to point your webcam at it). 8 - 10 small items to put on the tray.

Preparation Time: Less than 10 minutes.

Difficulty level: Easy for you to set up. Challenging for them!

Wacky Races

Most kids will respond to challenges when they're up against the clock and that's as true for everyday parenting as it can be for video-calls. Just be careful not to use this trick too often doing things that aren't much fun like tidying their rooms, or they'll start to associate the idea of racing against the clock with things that they don't like to do.

When should you use the clock? How about a picture drawing race... Who can draw the most things to do with 'summer' in under 5 minutes? Once you are both ready with your materials, you start the clock and show each other what you have done after 5 minutes. If your kids are of reading and writing age, try the same format but with words rather than pictures: 'How many words can you think of that remind you of the Zoo?' for example.

Because my children live together, I sometimes suggest a race between them, which again can really be about anything! For example, who can find the most interesting 3 things to show Daddy the quickest? When they return from looking, ask them to explain why they think what they found is so interesting. This is a great way of getting their brains whirring and making meaningful contact.

Tips: With two or more children be a bit careful about what kind of race you choose. Kids can be competitive and it's always best to try and avoid arguments and tears!

Resources: A stopwatch is handy, but if they're near to finishing their rabbit and the clock says 5 seconds to go, put the clock away and let them finish their drawing while you slowly count down 5 - 4 - 3 - 2 - 1!

Preparation Time: Less than 5 minutes.

Difficulty level: Easy

Go to an Art Gallery or Museum

Art galleries and museums around the world have embraced the digital era and opened their doors to all sorts of great Art and artefacts online, so why not take a virtual tour of the ancient Egypt at the British Museum? Or check out some Van Gogh Art paintings at Amsterdam's Van Gogh museum? Ask questions about the things you find together, and find out where they would like to go next on your journey together.

Tips: The Van Gogh Museum has a great children's section with a stories section and colouring pages to print off and enjoy together. If you have a museum or gallery near where you live (or where they live) why not visit their online gallery and then go together in real life on your next visit? This is a great way of integrating your 'online' and 'real life' experiences to make things feel more real.

Resources: Screen sharing software such as Skype or Google hangouts, and a laptop or desktop computer for the best experience on your side.

Preparation Time: Less than 5 minutes.

Difficulty level: Easy

Un-contacted Tribes

This one is interesting for kids and adults, with the exception perhaps of the under 5's.

If you are unaware of the world's 'un-contacted tribes' you might want to do some homework before calling to school up on the subject.

When you are ready, open an internet browser and type into your search engine 'un-contacted tribes'. The top results will tell you all you need to know about this fascinating subject. After that, you will need to pick and choose the images and video you would like to show your children - best to do this before-hand as some images and videos may not be suitable for young children.

Now start the call and share your internet browser screen to show them what you found. No doubt your children will be fascinated by the images and video of Amazonian Indian people covered in body paint and holding spears and bows and arrows, or Papuan tribespeople with feathers in their hair and bones through their noses.

Ask your children what they think about these strange looking people. Show them the huts that they live in. Ask them why they might be carrying spears and other weapons? Ask them to imagine life without cars and computers and even simple things that we take for granted like a toothbrush or a mirror. There are very few un-contacted tribes left in the world, so ask your children if they think it's a good idea for us to make contact with these people or not, and why?

Tips: When you've finished, you might like to ask them how many un-contacted people they think there are in the world - we don't know for sure, but around 10,000 is a fair guess. Then ask how many people live in the rest of the world and show them the world population clock - approaching 8 billion at the time of writing this second edition.

Resources: A desktop computer for screen sharing.

Preparation Time: Less than 5 minutes if you are tech-savvy. Add 15 minutes if not.

Difficulty level: Easy / Medium

Hangman

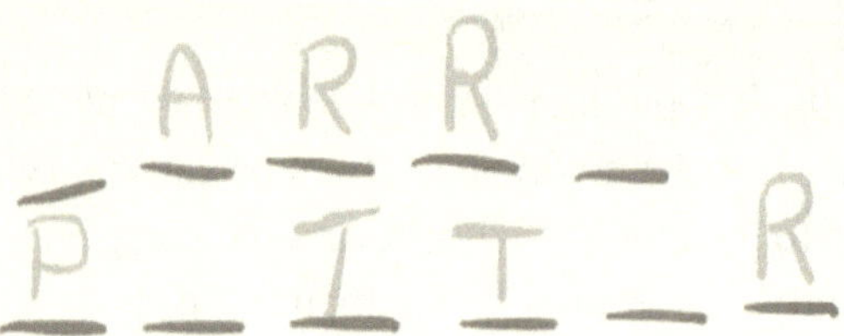

Hangman is very popular with my kids for video calls and it's very easy to do using the screen sharing feature, so let's get stuck in…

Start by googling 'Hangman for Kids' and try a few different websites until you find one that you like - www.hangman.org.uk is our favourite with plenty of different themes including 'animals', fruit and vegetables', 'boys and girls names', 'capital cities' etc. There's even a Harry Potter theme which they love!

Now start your call and use the 'share a window' feature to begin the game!

Tips: Take it in turns to choose a letter and don't be afraid to help out and give clues here and there!

Resources: A desktop or laptop machine on your side for screen sharing.

Preparation Time: Less than 5 minutes.

Difficulty level: Easy.

Water Gel Beads

Ideally this activity should be undertaken some time after you've done 'Giant Gummy Bears' as it is a similar concept, and follows on quite nicely, especially if you start involving plant material.

Start by ordering two sets of Water Gel Beads ahead of time, one for you and one for your kids.

During your next Skype session, after you have both received the beads, ask the children to find a large plastic cup or container (preferably clear so that they can see inside) and fill it 1/2 to 3/4 full of water. Now pour the beads into to water and out the container safe until the next video call…
By the time your next session comes around, your gel beads will have grown to the size of marbles! Drain the remaining water from the container and ask your child to put their hand in to see what it feels like?!

No doubt they will want to make their own fun with the beads, but a great educational activity to try is to take flowers, or a cutting and plant it in the container. A cutting will grow roots, and flowers will survive longer because of the water held in the beads.

Tips: The gel beads are small in their dried form and have a tendency to go everywhere if spilled, so this activity may need some adult supervision.

Resources: Water gel beads (cheap and easy to purchase online from retailers like Amazon or Ebay). Plant cutting if you decide to try to grow something!

Preparation Time: Beads need to be purchased and sent to kids ahead of time.

Difficulty level: Medium.

Balloons

Plain old party balloons can work great for video-calls, and of course they come in all shapes and sizes which means you can surprise your little ones by not showing them what shape yours is before you inflate it. When I use balloons I always make sure I've got a permanent marker pen to hand so I can draw a big heart and kisses, and write 'Love Daddy' on the balloon once it is blown up. When you've finished with the pen how about pulling the neck of the balloon between your thumb and index finger on both hands to make a squealing noise? Or try asking the kids to count-down from 5 and let the balloon go flying around the room.

Tips: When you're done with the balloons don't throw them away - put them to one side and next time you send your kids a parcel in the post you can put the balloons inside too for them to blow up!

Resources: If you're feeling adventurous and want to try making the animal shapes you see at fairgrounds, you're going to need special #260 balloons which are available from most party stores. Instructions on how to make them are readily available online.

Preparation Time: Less than 5 minutes if you already have balloons.

Difficulty level: Easy. Medium if you try to make animal shapes with #260 balloons.

Computer Games

If your children are old enough, computer games really are a great way of connecting with them at a distance.

I realised just how true this is when I watched my daughter running ahead of me in a game we were playing on Roblox. I was able to say 'wait for me' and she waited until I caught up. The interactions all happen in real time and you can still keep the conversation flowing via your video call, which makes the whole experience seem much more immersive and real, as if you are really there together, and that makes the all important 'connection' much more likely to happen!

Computer games also really help maintain the momentum of the call, as they usually have an aim which means that you can either collaborate or compete with your children, and maybe their friends too (see below).

Tips: Invite your children's friends or relatives to play too! I have played Fortnite with my son on my MacBook while he and his friend were on their Nintendo's, all of us in different houses in different parts of the world!

Resources: A device that can cope with the software you are using. Some mobile/cell phones are powerful enough to play Fortnite for example, but your best bet is a laptop/desktop or tablet for a decent sized screen, and the power to play without glitches.

Xbox Live and Nintendo Online enable more options for games like Minecraft and Fortnite too.

Preparation time: 15-30 minutes. You will need to make sure the Application/game you want to play is going to work on both sides. This is relatively easy if you both have the same game on the same device (Fortnite on Nintendo for example), but may be a bit more complicated across different devices and platforms. Roblox is a safe bet across different devices and can fun for younger children too.

Difficulty level: Medium. A bit of patience and coordination may be required to get set up.

Monster

This is a fun game that can easily be played on a video call. Perhaps you might end up with some great Artwork to send to each other at the end of it?!

The idea is to build a picture of a monster, bit by bit.

If your child is happy to start, ask them to describe what the monster's head looks like - is it big and round or long and narrow? As your child is describing the head you both start drawing your monster. Then you describe the monsters ears and your child describes the eyes and so on until you reach the feet.

By this time you should have a pretty amazing looking monster to show each other, so when you're ready count down from 3 and show each other your creations!

Tips: The more crazy the suggestions the better - make it fun! When you are finished, why not send each other your drawings in the post?

Resources: Colouring pencils, pens and paper (or a tablet, stylus and drawing app).

Preparation Time: Less than 5 minutes.

Difficulty level: Easy

Headgear

Stunningly simple, but always fun - wearing unusual hats, glasses or facial hair is always guaranteed to grab children's attention. So, for your next video call, grab the craziest looking garb you can find… Guys take a ladies hat if you can find one, and girls the opposite - maybe even a fake moustache if you can make one… Remember the crazier and more fun, the better!

Tips: If you are using Messenger, Snapchat, Facetime or Google Hangouts, why not try their 'Lenses' and 'Effects' - an awesome way to virtually turn yourself into a bespectacled professor, or a salty looking pirate with the click of a mouse button.

Resources: Raid your partner's cupboards, visit the dollar store or make your own.

Preparation Time: Less than 10 minutes if you have already have the gear. Add more time if you need to make your own or go shopping.

Difficulty level: Easy

Quiz

Quizzes are a great way of getting the kids brains working and their attention focussed, especially if you have more than one child.

I like to choose a quiz with a theme like 'animals', 'countries' or 'sports' but there are lots of other general quizzes that can be just as much fun.

Tips: I always try to give encouragement and praise to both of my children for the effort they make, and if one of them is dominating a little too much I'll try alternating direct questions between them so that only one person is allowed to answer at a time.

Resources: Quizzes are easy to find online by googling 'Quiz for kids', or you could do it the old fashioned way by purchasing a children's quiz book!

Preparation Time: Less than 5 minutes. Add more time if you don't want to use online quizzes.

Difficulty level: Easy for you to set up. Challenging for them!

Starting calls in unusual ways

One of the keys to consistent video calling is to keep things interesting - it gets boring for everyone if you're doing the same things all the time. And, one of the best ways that I have found to spice things up is to start Skype in unusual ways. Looking back through my Skype video recordings recently, I found a particularly good example which had the kids glued to the screen and in fit's of giggles...

First, I set the computer up facing an open window into the garden. Then I called the kids and ran outside with my iPad. When they answered, I paced back and forth looking at my iPad pretending not to hear their cries of 'Dad! Dad! Daddy!!!'. Then, when the time was right, I looked up in their direction and acted surprised to see them - 'Oh hello, I didn't see you there!' I said. By that time they were in hysterics of course and I had two attentive children for the rest of the session.

Tips: As with so many children's activities, let your imagination be your guide. If you have a cellular data connection why not go outside and see if you can find an unusual place to start your next session?

Resources: Depending on how adventurous you're feeling, a cellular data connection might be handy.

Preparation Time: Less than 5 minutes.

Difficulty level: Easy.

Bedtime stories

Depending on time differences and where you are in the world, bedtime stories are a great way for you to bond with your child at the end of the day.

Kids always like to look at the pictures in story books so if you are using a physical book and a tablet or cellphone, try flipping the camera around (or use a tripod - they're available for smartphones too) to show them what you're reading. If you are using a desktop or laptop, it's going to be a bit trickier but you've still some good options - how about sending them a copy of the book you are reading so that you can go through it together? This might help with their reading skills too?

The 'Share screen' option in Skype opens up still more (arguably better) possibilities for eBooks... With your book viewer application (Kindle, iBooks etc.) open, share your screen and start reading - your kids can read along and see the pictures too.

Lastly, if your kids are a bit older, how about reading them a book without pictures? If your kids get over-stimulated by screen time before bed, this might be a great option for you.

Tips: How about recording a story video and sending it to them in the post on a flash drive or DVD? Uploading it to Youtube is another option (don't forget that Youtube has a setting that allows you to only share videos with people you have shared the link with).

Resources: Books, eBooks and possibly a smartphone tripod (available for a few dollars from E-bay)

Preparation Time: Less than 10 minutes.

Difficulty level: Easy.

Nothing between the ears

Ever fancied trying your hand at magic? Well, now's your chance…

This activity is simple trick that will amaze your children if you do it properly, so best practice in front of a mirror before you start.

Grab something like a carrot or a banana and pass it from one hand to the other around the back of your head so it looks as though you are putting it in one ear and pulling it out the other. You'll need to rotate your head slightly in the direction of the hand holding the banana so that your child can't see your ear as you're passing it through. As you grab it with your other hand, rotate your head slightly in the other direction at the same time as they think you're pulling it out of the other ear. My daughter loved it and kept saying, 'That's amazing Daddy, that's amazing' until she managed to figure it out!

Tips: I screwed my face up and made struggling noises as I was pulling it out to make it seem real, and then I wiped the cellphone with a cloth because of all the brain-juice all over it… Ghastly, but fun!

Resources: You can use just about anything, but probably best not use anything too small in case your child tries to copy you and ends up with a pencil stuck in their ear!

Preparation Time: Less than 5 minutes.

Difficulty level: Easy, although you might want to practice in front of a mirror.

Old friends

Did your kids once live with you or near you? Or did they make friends with other children when they visited you last? If the answer is yes to either of these questions then why not try getting those kids involved in a surprise session? On one occasion I arranged for my friends daughter to sit in his swivel chair with her back to the computer.

When the call started we slowly swivelled the chair around... To reveal.... Their old friend who they were very excited to talk to!

Tips: While the old friends are all together, why not get them all involved in one of the other activities in this book?

Resources: an old friend!

Preparation Time: You need an old friend for this one, so however long that takes!

Difficulty level: Easy once the old friend is ready to go.

Hide and seek with toys

If you are on a mobile device like a tablet or cellphone, how about playing hide and seek? Hide the toy and then walk around the house (or garden) with the tablet asking the children to guess where it might be. As they get closer you say 'warmer', if they guess somewhere farther away, you say 'colder'…

Tips: Make sure you have wifi or cellular coverage in the place where you hide the toy! And why not take a photograph or screen-grab of the toy in it's hiding place to send to your child by email or hard-copy in the post to remind them of the game?!

Resources: A mobile device (preferably with a front facing camera).

Preparation Time: Less than 10 minutes

Difficulty level: Easy.

Interview a relative

This is a really cool way of involving older relatives in a group video call. The idea is that both you and the kids ask the older relatives about what life was like when they were young and maybe even what life was like for their parents and grandparents. What kind of car did they have? Did they even have a car? What were their favourite games? Did they have computers or the internet when they were young? If not, what did they used to do?! Where did they go on holidays, and what did they do there?

Tips: How about adding some cheeky curveball questions to your list like, 'Were the dinosaurs alive when you were a boy grandpa?'.

Resources: All of your participants must have the same application installed on their devices.

Preparation Time: Some organisational work to do ahead of time with this one. You need to find an interviewee and make sure their device is ready. You will also need to ask the kids to prepare a list of questions.

Difficulty level: Medium

Once Upon a Time

This one is dead easy and doesn't require any preparation time, so let's get stuck in.

The idea is that you're going to tell a story that you make up between you.

You start by saying, 'Once upon a time, there was a _________'

And your child says the next line telling us something about the '_________'. So for example,

Once upon a time there was an alien called Bob,
He had an orange face and bright blue ears.

You'll know when your story is running out of steam, but hopefully by that point you will have both managed to have fun flexing your story-telling skills.

Tips: How about recording your story and writing it down so that they can read it in the future? And how about your kids do the illustrations?

Resources: Your imagination! A call recorder if you are going to record the story. Paper and colouring pencils for the illustrations.

Preparation Time: Less than 5 minutes

Difficulty level: Easy.

Special Occasions

Birthdays, Christmas and other special occasions are all about fun, surprises and presents!... So you're going to need to be prepared for these special days.

I tend to make up a parcel of small, inexpensive, and lightweight things to send in the post including a card with a personal message to each child, balloons with things written on them, stickers, toy cars, glitter, etc.

I then use an online retailer to send larger more expensive items. This keeps courier costs low and guarantees that the items arrive there on time and in one piece.

When the big day arrives and you've started your call with a rousing rendition of 'Happy Birthday' or Jingle Bells, encourage them to blow up the balloons that you've written on, and blow some up on your side too, so that they can see you joining in the fun. If you're really well prepared you might even want to present a cake with candles on so that they can try blowing them out from their side! (you blow at the same time they do so the candles go out) The presents can then be opened and if things go well, you might even be able to ask about any plans that they have for the special day ahead!

Tips: Most retailers also provide an inexpensive gift wrapping service, including the option of being able to write your own gift tags, which comes in really handy.

Resources: Small, light gifts and cards to send in the post. An online retailer to send larger, heavier items.

Preparation Time: Lots! Planning is crucial with special occasions, so make sure you send your cards and packages well ahead of time.

Difficulty level: Medium. Once everything is organised the call should be easy and fun!

List of things to do for your next visit

This is an easy activity that may stretch over a few sessions as you start to think about the things that you'd both like to do during your next physical visit (or perhaps an extended video call).

If your child has already started to read and write, ask them to find a piece of paper and a pen and you do the same. As you are talking about all the exciting things that you would like to do next time, you both start compiling your list until…. Your next visit!

Tips: This is a great way of integrating your video calls with your real life contact and helps reinforce your children's understanding that the things you do on video calls happen in real time, in the real world.

Try to encourage fun quirky things like 'Eating an ice cream in the bath' - you don't want your list to become unrealistic and full of expensive trips to Disneyland!

Resources: Paper and a pencil, or Stylus and a tablet.

Preparation Time: Less than 5 minutes

Difficulty level: Easy.

Involving other people

Involving other people is a great way to mix things up and make the kids feel more involved and connected to your social world. This is particularly true of course, if they already know the people you're with.

My partner gets on great with my kids, so she'll often come over and get involved in whatever we're doing, which helps spice it up if things are getting a bit flat. She has great skills and experience with kids and is awesome getting involved with activities for my daughter. Family members are brilliant too because they can take over by themselves for a while which keeps things interesting and surprising!

If your family members aren't physically present, why not involve them in a group call?

But don't stop at family - I've even had fun Skype sessions with kids from the local park by showing my kids how far I can throw a frisbee. Both sets of kids thought it was really cool to be talking to other kids in a different country on a video call.

Tips: It goes without saying that involving complete strangers (other than younger kids) in your video call probably isn't a great idea - stick to friends and family, partners, neighbours and their kids.

Resources: other people!

Preparation Time: Involving other people generally takes some time to organise, so probably best not to leave this one until the last minute.

Difficulty level: Medium.

Visit the Zoo

Chimps, Flamingos, Rhinos, Hippos, Polar bears, Platipus… The list goes on! My kids and I visited the rhinos at Houston Zoo last time we went to the zoo, but there are lots of webcams at lots of zoos around the world, so wherever you are there will be animals to visit at any time of the day!

Tips: Why not have a drawing competition while you watch the animals? Who can draw the best chimp eating a banana?

Resources: 'Share screen' function on a software that supports it such as Skype or Google Hangouts.

Preparation Time: 5 minutes

Difficulty level: Easy.

Simon Says

An oldie but a goody! Simon says is a fun, simple game that works as well for video calling as it does in 'real life'.

Ask your kids to face the camera and wait for your command. When you start any sentence with, 'Simon says...' they must do whatever it is that you command them to do, for example 'Simon says, make a noise like a horse!'

If you do not start the sentence with 'Simon says...', the children must not do whatever you ask them to do. If they forget and do it anyway, they lose a life, or they're out of the game!

Tips: the sillier the better - use you imagination to come up with fun things for the kids to do. And how about switching it around so that your kids become Simon and you have to do whatever Simon says?!

Resources: A Simon (You!)

Preparation Time: Less than 5 minutes

Difficulty level: Easy.

Colouring, scrap and sticker books

Colouring is a simple activity that everybody is already familiar with. What you may not have considered is that colouring, scrap and sticker booking is a value-adding activity that has lots of advantages when it comes to video calls…

For starters, it focuses your child's attention on one activity in one place. Colouring and scrap/sticker booking is also a fairly passive activity, which means that you can ask them how school was today and other questions as you go along… And then when you get to the end, you can ask them to hold it up for you to take a photo, which makes them feel like they've done something awesome!

I like to get involved in colouring activities by asking my kids to hold their pictures up before we start; I then take a picture with my iPad camera, import it to my drawing application and colour at the same time as my son or daughter. At the end, we show our masterpieces to each other and talk about what we like!

Tips: An added bonus of this activity is that next time you send each other something in the post you can send your pictures too!

Resources: Colouring pens and sticker / scrap books are readily available from online retailers like Amazon if your child doesn't have some already. If you want to join in the colouring exercise on a tablet as I do, you'll nee a drawing application like Wacom's Bamboo from the App store, and a stylus (available cheap on Ebay)

Preparation Time: Less than 5 minutes, unless you need to go shopping!

Difficulty level: Easy.

Sing a song or a nursery rhyme

This is an easy activity that it guaranteed to liven up any video call. Even if you're not feeling at the peak of your game a little song can make all the difference. And with Youtube and other music based websites at your fingertips you've got all the backup you and the kids could ever need to pull off a rendition of your favourite nursery rhyme or song.

If you do need backup, load up your song and click play to sing along - the music will be transmitted from your computer's speakers into the microphone to their computer and vice versa.

You can of course mix this activity up with Musical Statues for extra fun!

Tips: Most songs and nursery rhymes are available on Youtube but you could always use your own music collection to do the same job.

Resources: Youtube or another music based website if you don't fancy going 'a cappella'!

Preparation Time: Less than 5 minutes

Difficulty level: Easy.

Come closer raspberries

Come closer raspberries is an easy and fun way of generating some giggles.

First of all you need to act like you have a big secret that you can't tell anybody… (well hardly anybody, except perhaps a responsible child who promises never to tell anyone else!). Now ask, 'Do you know anybody that can keep a secret?'. Of course the response is going to be 'I can keep a secret!'. To which you say, 'OK, well you're going to have to come close so that I can whisper it to you…. Closer… Still not close enough,' and then when they're really close, you say 'OK that's good'… Now, wait for a second or two to build the suspense… Then let a raspberry rip into the microphone!

Tips: Sometimes I'll mix it up by following the same routine but instead of a raspberry I'll make whispering noises, or monkey noises… This gets them excited so that next time they're not sure what noise to expect.

Resources: A tongue that can make good raspberry noises!

Preparation Time: None.

Difficulty level: Easy.

The Easter Bunny

Who would have thought drawing the Easter Bunny could be so much fun?!

My partner and I sat with my daughter and we both drew pictures at the same time. It was coming up to Easter, so my partner set about drawing an Easter bunny and I drew the grass with Easter eggs hidden here and there.

We discussed how many Easter eggs my daughter would like in the picture and then I hid an extra one behind a beautifully drawn butterfly … Well, that was it! "Where's the hidden one Daddy? Where is it?"

I told her that she could have a quick look now, but that she could look for it properly when she received it in the post. I turned the computer around and she eagerly looked all over for the Easter Eggs!

It must have worked, because next time we talked, the first thing she said was, "Daddy where's the Easter bunny picture?" - a sure sign that our session had gone well!

Tips: Use your imagination to create your drawing - how about drawing the top of an easter egg inside a kangaroo's pouch, or up a tree?!

Resources: Paper and colouring pens/pencils

Preparation Time: Less than 5 minutes, unless you need to go shopping!

Difficulty level: Easy.

Giant Gummy Bear

This is a 'time lag' activity, guaranteed to get kids excited about what might happen between this call and the next one.

All you need for it is a Gummy bear and a glass of water. If you can arrange for the kids to have one on their side too, all the better.

Now, when you're ready and you've built up a bit of suspense, drop the Gummy bear in the water and ask them to guess what is going to happen to it?! Asking questions like this gets them involved in the process of imagining different outcomes, which makes for good contact. The fun for them is in the expectation and excitement about what might happen next!

Tips: It takes a while (at least overnight) for the water and the Gummy bear to work their magic, so it's an activity that you can add towards the end of a session, as once you've dropped the Gummy bear in the water, there isn't much else to do apart from wait… And hope that they don't eat the bear!

Resources: A packet of Gummy bears (or equivalent) and a glass of water.

Preparation Time: Less than 5 minutes, unless you need to go shopping fo Gummy bears!

Difficulty level: Easy.

Photos, video and old scrapbooks

Photos, video and old scrapbooks are a great way of reminiscing over things that you've done in the past and reinforcing the bond that exists between you and your children. It works as well for video calls as it does when you're face to face.

The easiest way for you to share photographs and video from your side is to use the 'share-screen' feature. Fire up your photo or video application and start reliving those special moments. I recently replayed videos of us sledging in the snow which my daughter really enjoyed.

Another scenario for this activity is for you both to have a physical copy of the same photo book, which you can arrange to be printed and delivered online.

When it comes to scrapbooks on their side, ask them to share their thoughts and memories by holding their pictures up to the camera (most kids cotton on to how to do this pretty quickly).

Tips: There are lots of online photographic retailers these days offering photo-book printing services - simply upload the photos (jpegs of drawings) to their web-servers, and choose which format and size you'd like for your book. Then print two copies - one for you and one for the kids!

Resources: Photographs (electronic or physical), video and scrapbooks.

Preparation Time: Less than 15 minutes, unless you are buying hard copies of photo albums.

Difficulty level: Easy.

Rhyme Time

No props required for this one - just a tongue that can rhyme, and a you'll do just fine.

The idea is that you'll be building a poem or a rhyme together, line by line. The adult starts first and the child follows with something that rhymes. If they are struggling, then give them a hand and encourage them to think of words that rhyme with the keywords in your sentence.

Limericks are an ideal format for kids, they're silly, fun and only 5 lines in length. If you're struggling for ideas, try googling 'kids limericks' and go from there. They usually start something like this;

There was a young girl with green hair,
(next line)… that lived in a lion's lair!
and so on...

Tips: The sillier it is the more fun it will be!

Resources: Just your imagination (or you can cheat a little bit by getting your ideas from limerick websites)

Preparation Time: Less than 5 minutes.

Difficulty level: Easy. If you're not much of a poet, use online limericks.

The On / Off Switch

You'll know immediately if you are pushing the right buttons with your child on a video call - their look changes and there's a sparkle of interest in their eyes. And it can come from anywhere, so let your imagination play along with your child and see where it leads you... The other day, my son was getting distracted by what the rest of the family were up to in the other room. I tried to get his attention in all the normal ways but nothing was working... So I turned my video off, but kept the sound on and kept quiet... After a minute or two, my son looked at the screen and said 'Dad? Dad where are you? Are you there' ... I kept quiet for a few seconds longer and then said, 'I'm still here, but I'm only going to turn my video back on if you can find me something really interesting.' He immediately went off to find a tractor that he had made out of Lego, I turned my video back on and we settled into a conversation about his tractor.

Tips: You wouldn't want to use this trick too often, but now and again it might just perk things up!

Resources: No special props required for this one :)

Preparation Time: None.

Difficulty level: Easy.

My Word

My Word is a game where cards are dealt face up on a table or the floor in front of you. The cards have one or two letters on them and the idea is to make up words from the selection available. It works really well with video calls and my kids love it!

Start by angling your laptop or webcam so your children can see the playing area and then begin turning the cards over for them to see. Your kids will start shouting out words as they see them and it's your job to check whether there are enough letters for the words they suggest. Add the letters from valid words to a pile for each child and perhaps one for yourself and the winner is the one with most cards!

Tips: If there are 2 or more children involved you may find yourself playing the role of peace keeper at times, as kids can get excited and competitive playing this game!

Resources: Although My Word can be purchased online, you could easily make you own version of the game if you are feeling creative.

Preparation Time: Less than 5 minutes, unless you need to go shopping for the game.

Difficulty level: Easy.

Telling stories about your time together

Talking about things you have done together in the past, is a great way of reinforcing your relationship with experiences that you can both remember and maybe even laugh about. I used to swing my children around in the bottom of a sleeping bag before launching them onto the bed, which they used to love - whenever I remind them about it now, they get excited and ask if we can do it next time I see them in person!
Reminiscing with stories like this also reminds them that you don't just exist on a computer screen but in real life too.

Tips: this activity doesn't need to be just about physical contact - why not talk about some of the fun things you have done together on video calls also?

Resources: scrapbooks, photos and diaries are all useful to refer to when trying to remember the things you have done together.

Preparation Time: Less than 5 minutes.

Difficulty level: Easy.

Treasure Hunt

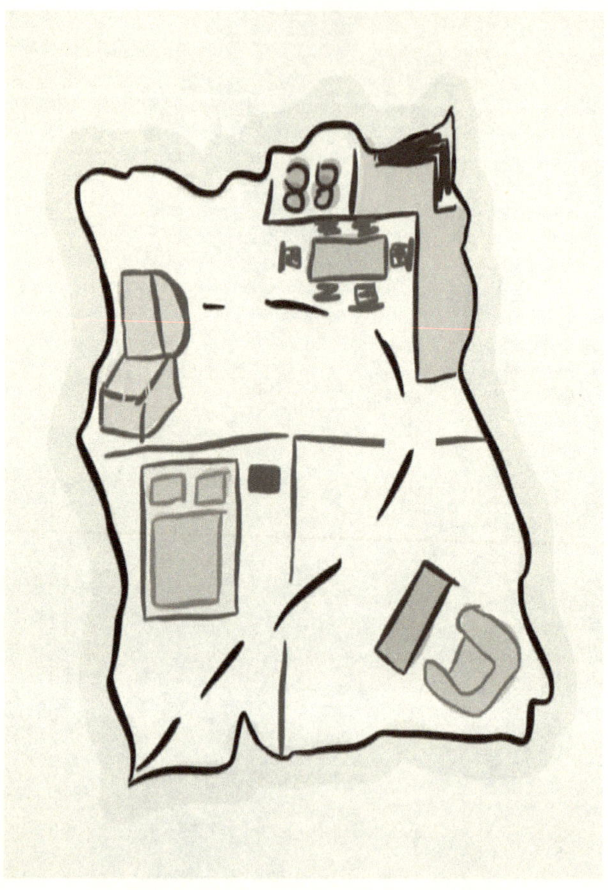

This activity is like a more complicated version of 'Hide and Seek with Toys', with clues and a gift at the end of the treasure trail.

Hide the clues written on small pieces of paper around your house (and maybe your garden too) and then walk around with your tablet asking the children to guess where the first clue might be. When they find the first clue, read it out loud so they can guess where you need to go next.

The first clue could be under the pillow on your bed, and it might read 'We need one of these to drink out of when we get thirsty' (a cup in your kitchen). The next clue might read, 'we put this on our toothbrush when we clean our teeth in the morning and before bed' (under a tube of toothpaste). .. And so on until they find the gift that you are going to send them in the post!

Not only is this a fun activity guaranteed to keep them interested, but it is also a great opportunity to show them, or remind them of where you live!

Tips: Check to make sure you have wifi or cellular coverage in the places where you hide your clues and gift before you start the call! And why not take photographs of your hiding places to remind them of the game during your next session?!

Resources: A mobile device such as a cellphone or tablet.

Preparation Time: 30 minutes or less.

Difficulty level: Medium.

Two way Jenga

We stumbled upon this one by chance, and what a great session it turned out to be!

My son informed me that he would like to build a hospital for his toy soldiers from Jenga blocks and asked if I would like to build something too? Wow - our roles had been reversed with him suggesting an activity for us to do! It's great when this happens because it shows they are interested and involved, so if they make suggestions for things to do, try and go with it and your relationship is guaranteed to grow.

When we had finished building our hospitals, we used the left-over blocks to make a tower, and played Jenga, until… You guessed it, Dad lost!

Tips: you can play this any way you want to of course - you can play straight up Jenga or maybe you can ask your child what they'd like to build and you build it together as we did!

Resources: two sets of Jenga blocks - one for you and one for your playing partner. Jenga blocks (or equivalent) are readily available from most online retailers and toy outlets.

Preparation Time: Less than 5 minutes, if you both have Jenga blocks already.

Difficulty level: Easy.

Cups and coin trick

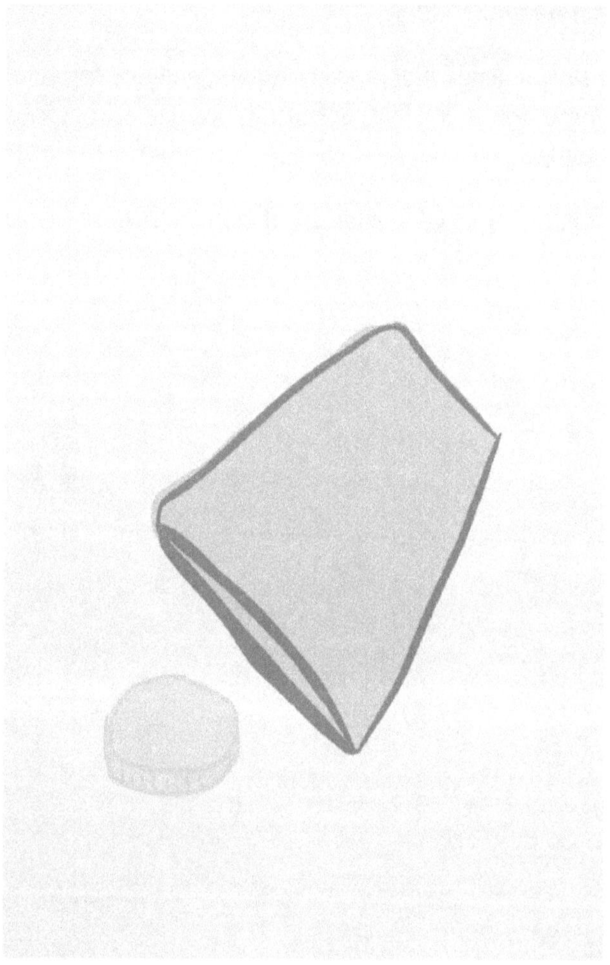

This is an old one that works as well for video calls (if not better) as it does in real life.

Place a coin on the table in front of you along with three upturned cups. Angle your webcam so that the kids can see what you're doing with the cups. Now, put one of the cups on top of the coin trict and ask the children to keep watching the cup with the coin underneath it. Start shuffling the cups slowly to start with and then faster. Now stop and ask your child/children to guess which cup has the coin underneath it!

If you're not the best cup-shuffler and the kids are on to you every time, try moving the webcam to focus on your face while you're doing it and ask them the question, 'Are you watching carefully?' then move the webcam back into position, they may cotton on to what you're up to, but it might make the game more fun!

Tips: Try moving the cup with the coin under it to the edge of the table and letting the coin fall on the floor - when they come to guess which cup it's under they will be amazed when you show them that it has disappeared!

Resources: A coin (or anything else that will fit under a cup) and 3 cups that look the same.

Preparation Time: Less than 5 minutes.

Difficulty level: Easy.

Watching a Show Together

Now and again, you might find this activity useful but be careful how you use it - after all, good contact is about making connections and having fun together, not vegging out in front of the TV!

 'Share screen' makes it possible for them to watch whatever you're watching, so how about finding a copy of their favourite show and watching it together?

At the end, ask them questions about what they enjoyed most and why? Tell them what you thought was fun, and rewind to the best bit's to play them again, especially if there was lots of laughter!

Netflix has also recently added 'Netflix Party' as a Google Chrome extension, making things even easier, but you will be have to be a Netflix subscriber to take advantage of it, and you will be restricted to shows that are on Netflix.

Tips: Why not try watching a film together over a number of sessions? Harry Potter is very popular with my kids!

Resources: A copy of their favourite show, on DVD, hard drive or online. Open it up in a windows on your computer and share via Skype! Simple as that.

Preparation Time: 10 minutes or less, unless you need to go shopping for their favourite show.

Difficulty level: Easy.

Magic Trees

Kids love watching things grow and change, so this is another great time lapse activity that you can start during one Skype session and carry over to the next.

Send them a Magic Tree kit in the post and ask them if they know what crystals are?!

When you're ready to start, ask the kids to open their kit's and place their cardboard cut-out tree into the saline mixture. What do they think is going to happen? How do they think the liquid will change their tree? Now ask them to put it somewhere safe, and by the time your next session comes around you'll be able to talk about what has happened and perhaps some of the science behind it!

Tips: Depending on the age of the child, a little bit of adult help might be required with this one.

Resources: Magic Trees are available to buy online for not very much money at all or you can make them yourself - again instructions are available online.

Preparation Time: They will not have Magic trees ready to go, so you'll need to send them kit's ahead of time.

Difficulty level: Medium. Help may be required on their side, depending on how old your children are.

Spelling and maths

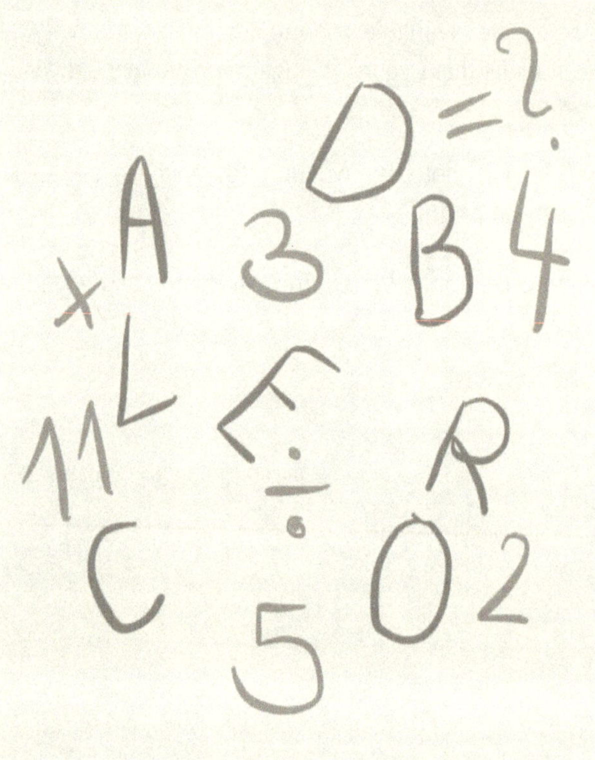

Generally speaking, this activity will be appropriate for younger children starting school, but kids develop at different paces, so tailor this activity to suit them.

Take letters from the alphabet and arrange them on a tray or table and then ask your child to read the words you have created. Why not create themes, like animals, or fruit, or capital cities?

My daughter is big on maths, so how about doing the same with numbers? Create simple (or not so simple!) equations starting with 4+3=? and go from there.

This activity can be alternated with My Word, where kids make up words from a collection of random letters.

Tips: Why not turn this activity around and ask your children to create words and themes for you to look at - this will help them develop their spelling skills and confidence presenting their ideas to other people!

Resources: Fridge magnet numbers and letters are useful for this activity but anything will do - you could use MyWord cards or handwrite and cut out your own letters.

Preparation Time: 10 minutes or less, unless you need to go shopping or make your own numbers and letters.

Difficulty level: Easy.

Musical Statues

If you've never played musical statues before, let me give you a quick 101 - it's very easy!

1) Start the music.

2) Turn the volume down slightly and tell the kids that when the music stops they're going to have to be completely still like a statue. Only breathing and blinking allowed.

3) Stop the music for a while and make sure everyone is still.

4) Start the music again.

If you have two or more children playing the game, how about a competition where anyone that moves when the music stops loses a life or is out of the game. The winner is the last child standing!

My son's favourite music at the moment is 'Gangnam Style' - perfect for getting them going and for dancing during and after the game. My daughter's favourite is the music from the movie Frozen which is guaranteed to get her singing along.

And don't forget that you can always share your screen or use an iPad or a phone to show them the videos that go with the music after the game.

Tips: How about prizes sent in the post for the winners and runners up?

Resources: You don't need a separate music player to do this - your device's speaker should be enough to play the music which will then get picked up by the microphone for the kids to hear.

Preparation Time: Less than 5 minutes.

Difficulty level: Easy.

Squeaky voice / Darth Vader Voice

Using 'voice changer' software it's possible to make your voice high pitched and squeaky, or deep and low like Darth Vader!

On your side, everything will still seem the same, but on their side every time you say something your voice will be filtered through the app and you'll sound completely different!

In order to get things going you'll need to download and configure your software of choice, then make the call and let the fun begin!

Tips: This activity might not be for everyone. Setting things up can be a little frustrating and a bit technical depending on the computer and software you are using.

Resources: A desktop computer and voice changing software. I used Garageband and Soundflower on my Mac, but this was tricky to set up. Also, software evolves quickly, so my best advice here is to google 'Skype/Google Hangouts Voice changer' to find out what suit's your budget and computer.

Preparation Time: Depending on the technology, preparation time may vary a lot, and could be up to an hour.

Difficulty level: Can be tricky to set up.

Paper Planes and Origami

Making paper airplanes and origami figures is a great way of focussing your child's attention whilst making something together. Much like colouring, it keeps their attention in one place and you're able to ask them a few questions about how their day was along the way.

Boys love airplanes generally and origami figures of boats and birds works great with both boys and girls but mix it up and see what works for your child.

The key to making this work successfully is setting things up correctly and being patient!

Start by making sure that you both have your paper ready, then angle your web-cam or laptop lid so that your child can see what you're doing. Start with something basic like a paper airplane and show them slowly, step-by-step how to make it.
Remember to be patient - it might take a few sheets of wasted paper before your child gets on the right track but whatever they end up with will be brilliant, right!? Once you have managed to coordinate success on both sides with a basic plane, why not try getting a bit more adventurous with an origami boat or bird?

Tips: Colouring pens and stickers at the ready...? How about decorating your creations and sending them to each other in the post? Receiving something in the post reassures your child that Skype calls happen in the real world and in real time, not just on a computer screen.

Resources: A ream of standard A4 paper and if you are not a paper plane or origami guru don't worry, it's not that hard and there are lots of resources online to show you how.

Preparation Time: Less than 10 minutes.

Difficulty level: Easy / Medium.

Dead or Asleep?

Dead or Asleep is a great way of grabbing kids attention. It's very easy to do and works as well for video calls as it does face to face.

On one occasion whilst driving, I stopped the car, perched my laptop on the dash board, put my seat back and closed my eyes. When the call started I pretended to be asleep. At first I made light snoring noises, gradually getting louder and louder, until I heard the children starting to whisper to each other 'Dad's asleep'… I then 'woke up' and said 'Oh, hello, how long have you been there for?'… And off we went.

Of course I could not see their reactions at the time, but upon playing the recording back, I could see them giggling and whispering to each other, thinking that I was fast asleep in the car!

Playing dead is another age-old way of grabbing kids attention, and crops up often during a gunfight with my son! It's also a good way for adults to catch their breathe if things are getting a bit crazy ;)

Tips: Dead or Asleep can be done anytime, anywhere. Use your intuition and if you notice their attention wandering or if you fancy starting your call in a different way, why not give it a try.?

Resources: A healthy snore, and a cellular data connection if you want to try it in the car.

Preparation Time: None.

Difficulty level: Easy.

Shoot-outs

This activity could become an old standard for you as time goes on. I always keep a couple of toy guns in the drawer ready to pull out at a moment's notice… (usually after my son has appeared on screen shooting me with a huge noisy bazooka!)

You can pretty much go with the flow when it comes to gun fights, but if the action gets a bit slow, try mixing things up by hiding behind something, and then popping your head out to give your child a chance to shoot when you appear!

Tips: If your gun doesn't make noises, try googling for a gun-noises website that you can use when you're playing… (the noises coming out of your speakers should feed back into the microphone as you're playing). One that I found has a wide variety including gun-cocking noises and ricochet sounds which can be quite fun when it's high noon!

Resources: Guns are available from toy retailers. For gun noises try - http://soundbible.com/tags-gun.html

Preparation Time: Less than 10 minutes.

Difficulty level: Easy.

Strange noises

One day, as part of something else that I was working on, I downloaded some recordings of bird sounds. When I found things getting a bit slow during a subsequent video call with my son, I played some of them while we were talking. Soon enough he pricked up his ears, smiled and looked directly at me, asking 'Where are those bird sounds coming from?'. To which I replied, 'What bird sounds?'… He smiled an even bigger smile and said, 'Those bird sounds!', looking out of the window,. 'Maybe they're coming from your garden?' I said. But he's not stupid and soon figured out that I was having him on, 'They're coming from the computer!' he said.

Children are always intrigued by something unusual. Getting their attention by playing unusual noises or showing them interesting things is always a good starting point for meaningful contact.

After our session that day, I suggested that to my son that he might listen out for some bird sounds when he went outside… Perhaps he might recognise some of them?

Tips: It's always fun to play along and feign ignorance when you're goofing around with kids. It makes for a bit of pantomime, and usually winds up with a good laugh.

Resources: There are plenty of noises that you can use to pique your child's attention, but if you like the idea of birdsong try www.soundbible.com/tags-bird.html or www.freesound.org/browse/tags/birds/

Preparation Time: Less than 5 minutes.

Difficulty level: Easy.

Section 3

Outdoor Calls

From going for a bicycle ride, to Geocaching, there's lots to do outside...

Introduction to outdoor calls

Outdoors video calls can be a really fun way to interact with kids. Sessions typically begin with their undivided attention and lots of 'where are you?' questions before we move into whatever it is we're going to do.

Playing with their curiosity is a great way to start any session, and the opportunities are endless when you're outdoors. For example, we live near a big, beautiful lake, so on one occasion at sunset, I set the laptop up facing out over the lake. As soon as the call started, I stood behind the laptop with some sticks, and waited… 'Daddy… Daddy…?! Daddy?!?' And then a big 'Splosh' as I throw a stick into the water… 'Daddy, what was that?… Look I can see ducks… Daddy?!?' Splosh… Daddy, where are you?! And then I go in front of the camera and say a big HEEELLLLLOOO!!! By this time, the kids are so magnetised by what you're doing, that it feels like the barrier of distance has evaporated, and they're there with you by the lake… Whatever you do next, whether it is to jump into the lake, or look for wildlife, you're guaranteed good contact and a fun session!

Resources:

I use my mobile phone to set up a Wifi hotspot that my laptop or iPad can connect to. This is easy to do… A bit of googling and you'll be set up in no time.

Remote Control Parent

I recently had an outdoor video call where I held my laptop in front of me and asked the kids to direct where we should go… The result? They were immediately interested and involved! 'LEFT' shouts my daughter… 'RIGHT' shouts my son… 'Straight on?' I ask… Yes, straight on, no LEFT!' … 'What's that over there?! Go there!'…

While they're directing you, keep an eye out for things that might be of interest. I found a group of children playing on the sports field and so we went and said hello. Look for fun stuff that is going to keep them and you amused. Is there a play park where you can sit on the swings? Are there animals or birds you can find? The possibilities are endless and that's what makes outdoors calls so good!

Tips: Even though I used a laptop on this occasion, a mobile device is much easier and more suitable for this activity.

Resources: Cellular data connection if you are out of Wifi network range.

Preparation Time: Less than 15 minutes.

Difficulty level: Easy.

Finding and eating Fruit and Vegetables

Foraging for fruit and vegetables is another outdoor activity that's guaranteed to keep them interested. It's fun, educational and focuses on healthy eating, so you can't go wrong!

Hold your mobile device in front of you and walk slowly towards the plant where your fruit or veg is growing. Ask them to guess what it is, getting closer and closer until they guess correctly, at which point you pick the veg and offer them some before eating it and telling them how tasty it is!

Offering kids to share what you're eating on video calls is not as silly as it sounds. They have fantastic imaginations, so joining in with food-tasting should be just as easy as holding a teddy-bear's tea-party!

Tips: IMPORTANT: Remind children that they should never eat anything which they have found whilst out foraging until they have checked with an adult that it is safe to do so.

Resources: You'll need a cellular data connection and a mobile device for this one. Then you'll also need somewhere outdoors to go foraging. This should be easy enough if you have a garden, but if not, perhaps the local park has some fruit and nut trees? If all else fails how about placing fruit and vegetables around your home and follow the same procedure by walking slowly towards them whilst they guess what it is?

Preparation Time: Less than 30 minutes

Difficulty level: Medium.

Geocaching

Geocaching, is an outdoor activity that involves looking for a container (geocache) that someone else has put in an interesting place. The boxes are sealed and usually contain a notebook diary for people to write in, as well as trinkets and small toys that people exchange for other things that they find in the box. The boxes are located using a cellphone or GPS device, and by figuring out clues left by the person who planted it. It's great fun for everybody, and they are usually found in places with something interesting to see or do like a great view for example, or an historic site.

Unless you live somewhere very remote there will undoubtedly be one near you, so get out there and enjoy a very different kind of video call!

Tips:

- You might want to go out and get an idea of where the Geocache is prior to calling - sometimes they can be quite hard to find and if you are using the GPS function of your cellphone you might find it tricky to maintain a call at the same time as using the Geocache App.

- How about talking to your kids about Geocaching prior to your big adventure? Show them maps using 'share screen' to work out how you are going to get to where you need to go.

- Ask them what they would like you to take with you to put in the box, and send them whatever they choose to swap for it.

- When you find the geocache be sure to write in the diary that you found it with your children on that day and take a photo to send to them.

- On one occasion I made a geocache with my kids. If you are feeling really adventurous, why not do the same? Perhaps they could send you some pictures, messages and a small toy or two to include in the box. If you do decide to have a go at this, make sure you do a follow up session a few months later to see who has discovered your box.

Resources: First of all you'll need to find a Geocache near you. This can be achieved by using one of the Geocaching services available online. Geocaching.com is the most popular, boasting more than 2.6 million Geocaches worldwide and a mobile app for use with the GPS function of your cellphone. You'll also need a cellular data connection and a mobile device with a front facing camera (most modern cellphones and tablets have this functionality)

Preparation Time: Up to an hour or more to set up software and devices.

Difficulty level: Fine after initial setup which can be tricky.

On the lake

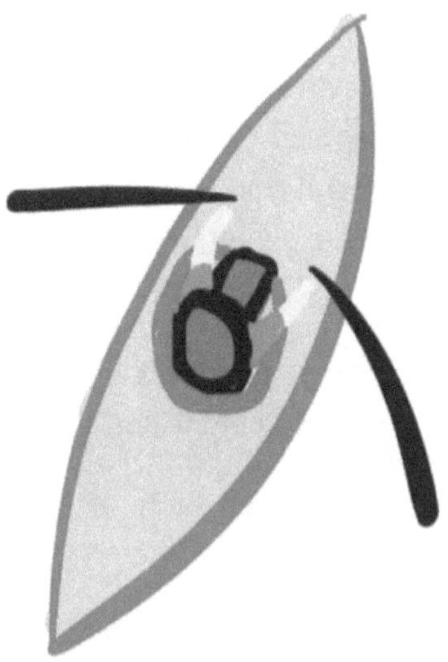

This one is really about thinking outside the box... Remember that now and again, it helps to keep things interesting by doing something a bit different. If you live somewhere hot, then outdoor calls are something you can get creative with at any time of the year, otherwise it's mostly going to be a summer thing.

We are lucky enough to have a big lake nearby, so one summer evening my partner and I took the kayak down to the lake for a Skype session. I got in the kayak and paddled out a meter or two and then asked my partner to dial the kids. When they answered, their computer screen was filled with the image of me in a kayak on the lake... They were instantly glued to the screen, asking questions incessantly! After a minute or so, I paddled closer and took the mobile phone from my partner and paddled one-handed out a little way into the lake, alternating between front and rear-facing cameras so that the kids could imagine themselves aboard the kayak with me. I also asked them which way to go, left or right or straight on - which is another great way of making them feel that they are right there with you… And it worked! My daughter was so 'into it' that at one point, after we had been out there for a while, she said, 'Daddy I want to go home now', to which my son replied, 'You already are home silly!'.

Tips: Chances are you won't have a big lake nearby, in which case try something different! Climb a tree and call them from the top or ask your partner to look for you in a crowd if you live in the city and then go for a walk with them. The possibilities are endless, so get creative and you're sure to make great 'contact'.

Resources: A mobile device and a reliable cellular data connection. A GorillaPod type tripod in case you need both hands free.

Preparation Time: Up to an hour, or more if you already have the equipment. Add more time if not.

Difficulty level: Medium.

Them Outdoors

On one occasion my daughter asked "Dad, can I show you my tricks on the trampoline?" - it's brilliant when kids take the initiative like this, so go with it!

She proceeded to turn the laptop around so that I could see the trampoline through the window. Once outside she climbed onto the trampoline and showed me all her best trampoline moves and because the trampoline was so close to the house she was able to see me clapping and cheering her every bounce!

Seeing this, my son wanted in on the action and asked if he could show me some of his soccer skills. "Of course, I'd love to see you playing soccer" I said, and we spent the next 10 minutes with him scoring goals and me cheering him on.

Tips: Video calls usually take place on a device that belongs to an adult, so it's really important to be mindful about how much manoeuvring it might take to get that device into position. Always ask the kids to check what you want to do is OK with the person who owns the device.

Resources: There are lots more possibilities if the children have access to a mobile device that they can take with them, but failing that a webcam pointing at the garden could be all you need to make this happen.

Preparation Time: Less than 5 minutes.

Difficulty level: Easy, as long as everything is working on their side.

Outdoor Surprises

Whether you're in your own back garden or roaming a local park on a cellular data connection kids love it when you mix things up to make video calls interesting. You might start by taking them to a place that they already know and zooming out from something close up until they're able to guess where you are?

And what about the places they don't know?! A zoo would be fantastic if you're lucky enough to live near one - imagine the fun that could be had by asking them which animal they'd like to find next, or the educational value of asking where in the world a Lemur or a Meerkat comes from?

The possibilities are endless… How about finding a cool car? Or a pony in a field? Use your imagination and remember that kids love surprise and suspense, so the more intriguing you can make it, the better!

Tips: You don't have to start off close to something and zoom out - you could do it the other way around by starting off quite far away from something and walk closer until they are able to guess what it is that you want to show them.

Resources: A mobile device with cameras and a reliable cellular data connection.

Preparation Time: Up to 30 minutes, or possibly more depending on what you plan to do.

Difficulty level: Medium.

Them outdoors on a mobile device

Being mobile opens up lots more possibilities for video calls than being tethered to a desktop computer. That's the same for the kids being mobile as it is for you.

A tablet with wi-fi connectivity is the perfect device for kids to take upstairs to show you their bedroom, or to go outside and show you what is living under a rock in the garden. Recently my son took his tablet onto the trampoline in the garden and we bounced away for about 10 minutes until we both felt queasy - him from jumping up and down and me from his camera bouncing from his face to the sky and back!

Tips: The options are only as limited as you and your child's imagination, so encourage your child to get creative and show you something exciting!

Resources: The perfect device for this one is a cheap wifi enabled tablet, which are readily available to order online for as little as around US$50. The tablet will still need the help of an adult to install apps like Skype safely, so make sure that's OK and that you are in agreement that your child is old enough for one.

Preparation Time: Less than 5 minutes, unless you need to go shopping for a mobile device.

Difficulty level: Medium.

Going for a Bicycle ride

If your cellular data connection is good and you're feeling adventurous, why not get out there and take the kids for a bike ride! The ideal place for this would be a public park or reserve that they may already know and recognise. Stop and show them things of interest that you see along the way. Maybe you could even take a picnic to break the journey up?!

Tips: Depending on how busy they are, cycle paths may be OK, but under no circumstance should you try this activity on a road used by other vehicles! Apart from being dangerous, it's going to set a bad example for the kids.

If you cycle too fast wind noise on the microphone will mean that your kids cannot hear you.

Resources: You will need a GorillaPod style mini-tripod for your mobile phone and hands-free earphones/headset. Wrap the tripod around your handlebars or attach to your bicycle helmet, connect your headset and away you go!

Preparation Time: Up to 30 minutes if you already have the gear.

Difficulty level: Medium / Difficult.

Sports Tricks

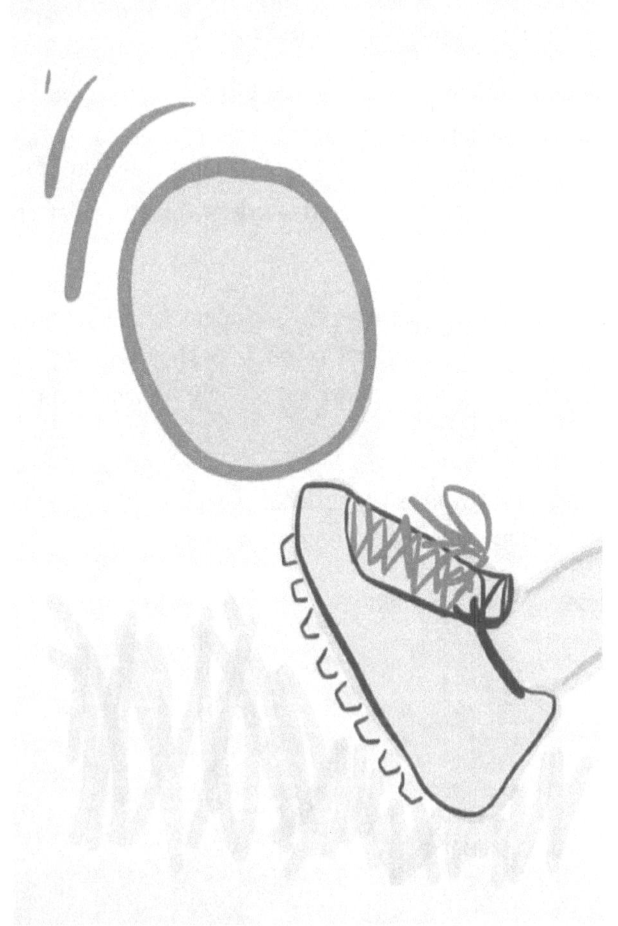

Showing off each other's sports skills is something that can work surprisingly well with video calls. All you need is some outdoor space (indoor sports tends to end badly!) and some sports equipment.

If your children are the ones doing the sports then you will need to be able to see them of course, which will probably mean a laptop pointing into their back garden - I've witnessed many a trampolining move, soccer goal and golf swing this way.

If you are the one doing the sports, then the only limit's are where your imagination (and mobile device) will take you. For example, I have started a video call by swinging a golf club in the distance, or throwing a frisbee to my partner whilst she stands behind a laptop on the floor.

Sessions like this remind them that you're not just a static face on a computer screen - you're a real person with arms and legs that plays sports just like they do, and on your next visit, you will have the added interest of being able to talk about 'that time when you scored a goal from the other end of the garden'!

Tips: If you have a frisbee, try setting up your device a short distance away, and throw it over the top (just try not to hit it!). They will see the frisbee coming towards them, but then disappear out of sight, to which you ask, "Did you catch it?".

Resources: Depending on who is doing what, you'll need sports equipment and possibly a mobile device with a cellular data connection.

Preparation Time: Less than 15 minutes.

Difficulty level: Medium.